CW01082108

HOW TO
SARS

REFUND
FOR SMALL
BUSINESSES

HOW TO GET A
SARS
REFUND
FOR SMALL
BUSINESSES

DANIEL BAINES

PENGUIN BOOKS

How to Get a SARS Refund for Small Businesses
Published by Penguin Books
an imprint of Penguin Random House South Africa (Pty) Ltd
Reg. No. 1953/000441/07
The Estuaries No. 4, Oxbow Crescent, Century Avenue, Century City, 7441
PO Box 1144, Cape Town, 8000, South Africa
www.penguinrandomhouse.co.za

First published 2019

1 3 5 7 9 10 8 6 4 2

Publication © Penguin Random House 2019
Text © Daniel Baines 2019

Cover image © Shutterstock.com

PUBLISHER: Marlene Fryer
MANAGING EDITOR: Ronel Richter-Herbert
EDITOR: Christa Büttner-Rohwer
PROOFREADER: Ronel Richter-Herbert
COVER DESIGNER: Sean Robertson
TEXT DESIGNER: Ryan Africa
TYPESETTER: Monique van den Berg

Set in 11.5 pt on 15 pt Adobe Garamond

Printed by **novus print**, a Novus Holdings company

Penguin Random House is committed to
a sustainable future for our business, our readers
and our planet. This book is made from Forest
Stewardship Council® certified paper.

ISBN 978 1 77609 425 7 (print)
ISBN 978 1 77609 426 4 (ePub)

Disclaimer

The information in this book is based on the law as it stood at the time of writing.
Tax laws are subject to frequent change. The tax rates are based on the figures given
in the Budget Speech delivered on 20 February 2019 and must still be passed into
law. This book is meant as a general guide and it is recommended that you seek
the advice of a professional for your particular circumstances.

To Jocelyn and Christian
And thanks to Mike Pasio for his assistance

CONTENTS

Introduction 1

Chapter 1: Types of business entities 3

1.1 Sole proprietorship 3

1.2 Partnership 4

1.3 Private company 5

1.4 Close corporation (CC) 6

Chapter 2: A short overview of business tax in
           South Africa 7

Chapter 3: Income tax for business entities 9

3.1 Basic principles of income tax for businesses 9

3.2 Taxable income 11

3.3 Deductible expenses 11

3.4 Wear and tear 13

3.5 Assessed losses 15

3.6 Tax rates 15

3.7 Dividends-withholding tax 21

3.8 Capital gains tax (CGT) 22

3.9 Provisional tax 23

Chapter 4: Employees' tax 31
4.1 Pay-as-you-earn (PAYE)............................. 31
4.2 Unemployment Insurance Fund (UIF) 32
4.3 Skills development levy (SDL) 33

Chapter 5: Small business corporations and
        micro businesses................................ 35
5.1 Small business corporations (SBCs)................... 35
5.2 Micro businesses 38

Chapter 6: Value added tax (VAT) 43
6.1 A short overview of VAT 43
6.2 Registration as a VAT vendor........................ 45
6.3 Advantages and disadvantages of registering as a
     VAT vendor...................................... 45
6.4 VAT-exempt and zero-rated supplies.................. 48

Chapter 7: Rental properties.............................. 49

Chapter 8: Tax returns and tax clearance certificates 55
8.1 Tax returns...................................... 55
8.2 Tax clearance certificates 56

Conclusion... 57
About the author 59
Reference list.. 61
Annexure A: Sample tax comparison for a company,
        sole proprietorship and small business corporation 63

INTRODUCTION

Running a business is not an easy undertaking. On top of your already heavy workload, you need to decide which type of entity you should use for running your business. This involves trying to understand the various tax implications of each type of entity.

How to Get a SARS Refund for Small Businesses explains in an easy-to-understand manner, and through practical examples, how businesses are taxed and what type of tax entity is most tax efficient for which type of business. In this book, I explain various types of tax that you may come across when operating a business, namely: income tax, provisional tax, capital gains tax (CGT), dividends tax, value added tax (VAT) and pay-as-you-earn (PAYE). An entire chapter is dedicated to the VAT system; here you will find out how it works and whether or not you have to register your business for VAT.

I also explain what the requirements are for a business to qualify as a small business corporation (SBC) or micro business to allow your company access to lower tax rates. In addition, a separate chapter explains the tax implications and means of minimizing tax for companies and individuals owning residential property that is let.

If you are thinking of starting a business or are already

running your own business, this book will significantly increase your understanding of tax issues, helping you deal with this vital aspect of running a business in an informed manner.

Chapter 1

TYPES OF BUSINESS ENTITIES

There are various types of business entities that individuals can use to run their business. The most common types of entities are:

- a sole proprietorship;
- a partnership;
- a private company; and
- a close corporation.

In the rest of this chapter, I provide a short overview of each type of business entity, as there are different tax implications for each one.

1.1 SOLE PROPRIETORSHIP

In a sole proprietorship, the owner trades in his or her own name as the sole proprietor of the business. The business is therefore not a separate legal entity from the business owner. The owner uses his or her own income tax number for the purpose of dealing with the South African Revenue Service, or SARS. When filling in a tax return, business owners will list the income and expenditure from the sole proprietorship as part of their income on their tax return. It is possible for a sole proprietor to have a normal salaried job and run a business as a sole proprietorship on the side; both sources of income will then be listed in that person's tax return and tax will need to be paid accordingly.

While a sole proprietorship is easy to set up – as there is no registration process or separate tax number – there are some distinct disadvantages to running a business as a sole proprietorship.

The main disadvantage of a sole proprietorship is the risk of personal liability of the business owner in the case of debt or insolvency. You may also be restricted in terms of access to capital, as many investors will only invest in a company.

A sole proprietor may employ staff and conclude contracts just as a company would. He or she can do so without the processes associated with a company (for example, having to sign directors' resolutions). A sole proprietor may not, however, pay themselves a normal salary that is subject to pay-as-you-earn tax (PAYE) from the sole proprietorship business. However, sole proprietors are entitled to take the profits of the business as their compensation from the business. The practical effects of this are dealt with later in this book. A typical example of a sole proprietorship would be a writer or a catering company.

1.2 PARTNERSHIP

Like a sole proprietorship, a partnership does not constitute a separate legal entity to its owners: it simply consists of two sole proprietors who have joined up to run a business together. The partners in a partnership will share in the profit or loss of the business. There will generally be a partnership agreement that deals with the percentage of profit or loss that each partner will be entitled to and the different obligations that each party has.

Partnerships can be useful if two people join their separate skill sets into one combined business. A partnership comes without all the legal requirements for a private company, but the partners are liable for the debts of the partnership business. A typical example of a partnership is a physiotherapist and a sports massage therapist who combine their skills to offer their clients both services.

1.3 PRIVATE COMPANY

A company that is registered for the first time will be a private company, or (Pty) Ltd. This private company is a separate legal entity from its owner(s) and has to be registered with the Companies and Intellectual Property Commission (CIPC). All private companies need to apply for an income tax number from SARS.

The person who sets up the company will, in most cases, become a shareholder and director of that company. The advantage of setting up a private company is that shareholders and directors are provided with legal protection from any debts the company may incur; as such, a company is a separate legal entity from the shareholders and directors. However, if a director of a company has traded in a reckless or fraudulent manner, this person may be held personally liable for the debts of the company.

While a company provides legal protection, it is more onerous to run than a sole proprietorship, as a company must comply with certain legal requirements that a sole proprietorship is not required to do. This is the primary disadvantage of opening a business as opposed to operating as a sole proprietorship.

An advantage is that the company may pay the directors a salary just as it would pay any other employee. However, a shareholder of a company may only receive dividends (discussed in Chapter 3) from a company and not a salary, unless the shareholder is also a director or an employee. A typical example of a private company would be a supermarket.

1.4 CLOSE CORPORATION (CC)

A close corporation (or CC) is very similar to a private company. Like a private company, a CC is a separate legal entity, but with members instead of shareholders. New CCs are no longer allowed to be opened and private companies may no longer be converted to CCs. By implication, CCs are becoming obsolete, and it is not recommended that business owners attempt to operate a business through a CC.

Chapter 2

A SHORT OVERVIEW OF BUSINESS TAX IN SOUTH AFRICA

All businesses in South Africa are required to register for income tax with the South African Revenue Service, or SARS. Upon registration, SARS will issue an income tax number to the business entity.

If you run your business as a *sole proprietor*, you should already have your individual tax number. You will therefore not be allocated a separate tax number for your business. Instead, you will be required to fill in all information regarding the income and expenditure of your sole proprietorship business on your individual tax return. This book will discuss in detail the difference in tax implications of running a sole proprietorship as opposed to a company, as they are taxed in very different ways.

The company that sets up and registers your business with the Companies and Intellectual Property Commission (CIPC) can also apply to SARS for an income tax number on behalf of the business. Note that, although you can register your company directly as an owner, it is sensible to have a professional company handle this for you, as there is a lot of paperwork involved that you will probably be unfamiliar with. It is also important to be aware that the process of obtaining a VAT number is separate to this and is not dealt with at the time of registering the business.

Businesses are potentially liable to SARS for the following types of tax:

- income tax;
- dividends withholding tax;
- capital gains tax (CGT);
- provisional tax;
- employees' tax (PAYE);
- the Unemployment Insurance Fund (UIF);
- a skills development levy (SDL); and
- value added tax (VAT).

These taxes will be covered in the chapters that follow. In the explanations, I emphasise the most important types of tax. This is why an entire chapter is dedicated to some types of tax, while others are best explained within the ambit of a chapter that deals with a particular type of tax.

Be aware of the fact that your business may not need to pay any of the above types of tax. For example, you will not pay income tax if your company has an assessed loss (see Chapter 3, section 3.5). Some types of tax, such as VAT, apply only once a business reaches a certain turnover, at which point the company is required to register for VAT (although a company may elect to register for VAT even if its turnover is less).

Not all taxes that are relevant to companies are covered in this book. However, the most common types of taxes are covered.

Chapter 3

INCOME TAX
FOR BUSINESS ENTITIES

3.1 BASIC PRINCIPLES OF INCOME TAX FOR BUSINESSES

Businesses are liable to pay income tax on any profits they have made. Businesses may deduct all applicable expenses incurred from income received to calculate their profit. Tax is then payable on this profit amount. Here is a basic tax calculation for businesses that provide a service:

Example 3.1 – Calculation for a business that provides a service
Gross income from services rendered: R10 000
Less deductible expenses: 5 000
Profit (taxable income): R 5 000
This business will therefore be taxed only on the profit made (R5 000).

The basic tax calculation for businesses that sell goods as a means of earning income will be slightly different:

Example 3.2 – Calculation for a business that sells goods	
Gross sales:	R10 000
Less cost of sales:	R 5 000
Gross profit:	R 5 000
Less deductible expenses:	R 2 000
Profit (taxable income):	R 3 000
This business will be taxed on the R3 000 profit made.	

All income that is received by a business forms part of its gross income, including gross sales in the case of a business that sells goods. Expenses are deducted from gross income to find the profit (taxable income).

There are, however, certain types of income that are exempt from taxation, such as certain government grants received. Companies – as opposed to individuals who may receive a variety of exempt income amounts – do not have many types of exempt income. For the purposes of this book, government grants are the primary type of exempt income for businesses. Government grants, such as the Export Marketing and Investment Assistance scheme (EMIA) from the Department of Trade and Industry, are useful ways in which businesses may receive tax-free income to grow their businesses. I recommend that all business owners look at the website of the Department of Trade and Industry as a starting point to determine whether they may be able to access any type of government grant.

All fees for services rendered and/or profit from goods sold will be subject to tax; i.e., they are not exempt income.

Let's briefly compare the calculations for a business in the above examples to the calculations for an individual who earns a salary. Any individual who is employed within a company will receive his or her monthly salary after tax has been paid over to

SARS by the employer. The amount paid to employees is the money they may use to pay for their monthly expenses. This is in contrast to a business that pays expenses first, then pays taxes.

In the remainder of this chapter, I explain in more detail the different concepts you should be familiar with when dealing with business taxes.

3.2 TAXABLE INCOME

Taxable income is an important concept, as a business only pays tax on its taxable income. Essentially, taxable income is the profit that the business has made – that is, gross income less exempt income and deductible expenses. Once the taxable income has been calculated, the amount of tax payable can be determined. Here is a basic calculation for taxable income:

Example 3.3 – Calculating taxable income	
Gross income:	R5 000
Less deductible expenses/exempt income:	R1 000
Profit (taxable income):	R4 000

3.3 DEDUCTIBLE EXPENSES

Certain types of expenses are deductible from a business's income. Expenses incurred in the day-to-day running of the business are deductible.

Common examples of deductible expenses include:
- rent for premises;
- salaries;
- director remuneration;
- telephone;

- internet;
- travel;
- printing expenses;
- rental of office equipment;
- stationery;
- cleaning services;
- marketing;
- insurance;
- security; and
- running costs of a motor vehicle used in the business.

It is very important to keep all invoices of expenses incurred for submission to SARS. The invoices must be kept for a period of at least five years after submission of the tax return. Other types of expenses are not deductible. Common examples include:

- personal expenses;
- purchase price of fixed property (except under certain circumstances – see section 3.4);
- purchase price of office equipment (this is deductible over a stipulated period);
- purchase price of motor vehicles (deductible over a stipulated period); and
- purchase price of computers (deductible over a stipulated period).

The general rule is that expenses that add to the assets of the business are not deductible, while expenses that are incurred in the day-to-day running of the business are deductible. Here is a more in-depth example of how to calculate taxable income, based on deductible and non-deductible expenses:

Example 3.4 – Calculating taxable income based on deductible expenses

Income from services rendered:	R200 000
Less rental expenses:	R 50 000
Less salaries:	R 40 000
Less security:	R 5 000
Less travel:	R 10 000
Less office equipment rental:	R 20 000
Taxable income:	R 75 000

3.4 WEAR AND TEAR

In the previous section I mentioned that some items that businesses have to buy are not deductible from income for tax purposes. Many of these can, however, be deducted over a stipulated period, usually over a certain number of years. For example, a laptop bought for business purposes may be deducted over a period of three years. The example that follows illustrates this:

Example 3.5 – Writing off an item over a stipulated period

Cost price of laptop:	R12 000
Write-off period:	3 years
Deduction per year:	R4 000

So a value of R4 000 may be deducted from the business income over three years.

Different types of items have different write-off periods. Periods range from 1 year (for items that cost less than R7 000) to 25 years (for a portable safe). Other common examples are:

- trucks: 3 years (heavy-duty) or 4 years
- passenger cars: 5 years
- drills: 6 years
- refrigerators: 6 years.

Here is an example of the effect of wear-and-tear deductions on taxable income:

Example 3.6 – Calculating deductions for wear and tear	
Gross income:	R200 000
Less deductible expenses:	R 50 000
Less wear and tear on laptop (value of R12 000):	R 4 000 (3-year write-off period)
Less wear and tear on fridge (value of R12 000):	R 2 000 (6-year write-off period)
Taxable income:	R144 000

Certain assets have their own special wear-and-tear allowances in terms of a specific section of the Income Tax Act No. 58 of 1962. For example, commercial buildings (new and unused buildings owned by the taxpayer and used in their trade for purposes other than residential accommodation) are allowed a deduction of 5% of the cost of the building per year. Other examples include buildings used by hotel keepers and aircraft. An unused building in a tax context refers to a building that has not been previously owned, i.e. a building that is bought directly from a developer. If someone buys a property from another person who has used it, they will not be entitled to this deduction.

3.5 ASSESSED LOSSES

If your deductible expenses exceed your income, you will have an assessed loss and no tax will be payable. This is best illustrated by means of an example:

Example 3.7 – Calculating assessed loss	
Income:	R100 000
Deductible expenses:	R120 000
Assessed loss:	R 20 000

There is no taxable income, so no tax will be payable.
The assessed loss is carried forward to the following year of assessment and can be offset against any taxable income in the following year.

Note that a salary is a deductible expense, so the employees' and directors' salaries can still be paid out even if there is an assessed loss. However, no dividends may be paid to shareholders (see section 3.7). A business may run for years at an assessed loss. There is nothing stopping this; the business will, in all likelihood, have cash-flow problems, however.

3.6 TAX RATES

Once the taxable income of a business has been established, the amount of tax payable can be calculated. This calculation will differ depending on whether the business is run as a company or sole proprietorship. In other words, the calculation to determine taxable income will be the same for companies and sole proprietorships; it is only once taxable income is established that the calculation differs.

Tax calculations for companies and CCs

Companies and CCs are taxed at a flat rate of 28% on taxable income. Here is an example to illustrate this:

Example 3.8 – Flat-rate calculation for companies and CCs	
Income:	R100 000
Less expenses:	R 20 000
Taxable income:	R 80 000
Tax at 28%:	**R 22 400** (28% of R80 000 = R22 400)

This company will therefore pay a total of R22 400 to SARS on a profit of R80 000.

Tax calculations for sole proprietorships

Individuals who operate their business as a sole proprietorship are taxed on taxable income at the same rates as individuals in salaried employ. Tax is calculated after the taxable income for the business has been calculated.

Example 3.9 – Taxable income calculation for sole proprietorships	
Business income:	R300 000
Less business expenses:	R100 000
Taxable income for the sole proprietorship:	R200 000

The taxable income of R200 000 is subject to taxation in terms of the individual tax tables. The individual tax table for the 2020 tax year is shown in Table 3.1:

Table 3.1 Individual tax rates – 2020 tax year

Taxable income (R)	Rates of tax (R)
0–195 850	18% of taxable income
195 851–305 850	35 253 + 26% of taxable income above 195 850
305 851–423 300	63 853 + 31% of taxable income above 305 850
423 301–555 600	100 263 + 36% of taxable income above 423 300
555 601–708 310	147 891 + 39% of taxable income above 555 600
708 311–1 500 000	207 448 + 41% of taxable income above 708 310
1 500 001 and above	532 041 + 45% of taxable income above 1 500 000

If your taxable income from your sole proprietorship business is R200 000 and you have no other taxable income, you will fit into the second band in Table 3.1. Your calculation will be as follows:

Example 3.10 – Calculating tax for a sole proprietorship	
R200 000 – R195 850	= R 4 150
R4 150 x 26%	= R 1 079
R1 079 + R35 253	= R36 332
Amount of tax payable:	**R36 332** (excluding any rebates applicable to individuals)

A sole proprietor does not need to register as an employer unless he or she has employees whose salary is higher than the tax threshold. Sole proprietors also do not pay PAYE each month (see Chapter 4, section 4.1 for further details on PAYE) on the amount they take from the sole proprietorship to live on. Each month, the individual calculates the profit he or she makes and takes the rest as a 'salary'. However, sole proprietors must remember to put a portion of their profit aside to pay for tax, when they file their provisional tax returns twice a year. All sole proprietors are provisional taxpayers (see section 3.9). In the above example, the tax to be kept aside is calculated as follows:

Example 3.11 – Calculating provisional tax to be kept aside	
Taxable income:	R200 000
Less tax payable:	R 36 332
Total 'salary' for the year:	R163 668 (R200 000 – R36 332)
Total 'salary' per month:	R 13 639

The individual will thus keep aside R3 027 per month for tax (R36 332 ÷ 12 = R3 027) and receive a monthly 'salary' of R13 639. This amount excludes individual tax rebates.

However, sole proprietors are entitled to a rebate on their tax liability. This is an amount by which a person's tax liability is reduced per tax year. It applies automatically to all individual taxpayers. In this example, the individual's tax liability of R36 332 will be reduced by a primary rebate (of R14 220 in the 2020 tax year). If this primary rebate is considered, the calculation will be as follows:

Example 3.12 – The effect of the primary rebate on tax liability	
Taxable income:	R200 000
Less tax payable:	R 36 332
Less primary rebate:	R 14 220
Total tax payable:	R 22 112 (R36 332 – R14 220)
Total 'salary' for the year:	R177 888 (R200 000 – R22 112)
Total 'salary' per month:	R 14 824
Total tax payable per month:	R 1 842 (R22 112 ÷ 12)

The tax liability will therefore be reduced from R36 332 to R22 112 for the tax year (R36 332 – R14 220 = R22 112). The sole proprietor would therefore keep R1 842 (R22 112 ÷ 12) aside per month to pay his or her provisional tax twice a year (see section 3.9 for a more detailed explanation of provisional tax).

Annexure A

Annexure A on pages 63 to 64 sets out four examples that show the different taxation implications for differently structured business entities. The same taxable income (R200 000) is used in all four examples to show the most tax efficient way of running a business that is earning taxable income to this amount.

Example A shows taxation calculations for a person who runs their business as a company but does not take a salary from the company. It shows a generally unrealistic scenario: unless this company is a side business, you will need to take a salary in order to pay for your monthly living expenses. However, it clearly shows the effect of not taking a salary and only receiving a dividend from the company after all expenses and taxes have been paid. In this example, the business owner would receive an amount of R115 200 in his or her pocket. Example B sets out a more realistic scenario: in this case, the business is run as a company and the owner receives a salary. Note that as a director, the business owner will receive a salary that is subject to PAYE each month. The profit that the company makes is then paid to the business owner as a dividend (after all taxes have been paid). Note that in this example, the business owner will receive an amount of R166 020 in their pocket from a combination of salary and dividends.

Example C shows the tax effect of running a business as sole proprietor. In this scenario, the business owner receives an amount of R177 888 in his or her pocket. While this amount is higher than in the case of a person running a company and receiving a salary and dividends, a sole proprietor does not have the legal protection that a company offers.

Finally, Example D shows the taxation implications of running a small business corporation (SBC). In this scenario, the business owner receives an amount of R177 220 in their own pocket. It is thus the best option of the four, as the owner receives the second highest amount after taxation, but also has the benefit of legal protection that comes with running their business through a company.

Based on the four examples in Annexure A, it can be seen that it is generally preferable to run your business as a company and pay a salary to the director as opposed to running it as a sole proprietorship. (While the net amount the director receives may be less, a company provides the owner with legal protection.) However, the running of a company does mean more administration and additional expenses. It will usually necessitate the hiring of an accountant to do the accounts and fill in the company tax returns. Therefore, you will need to determine carefully which option is best in your own circumstances.

It is also important to bear in mind that the scenario may change depending on the amount of taxable income that a business generates, and that these four examples do not cover all relevant tax implications.

Also keep in mind that if you are able to qualify as an SBC or micro business, these entities give you access to reduced rates of taxation compared to tax rates for a company or sole proprietorship (see Chapter 5 for more details on SBCs and micro businesses).

Tax calculations for a partnership

As a partnership does not represent a separate entity but merely two individuals working together, it is not taxed as a separate entity, as is the case for a company. Each individual in a partnership will need to declare the income and expenses from the partnership as well as their percentage of the partnership profit to SARS in their income tax return and provisional tax returns. Furthermore, they have to keep in mind that a partnership is treated as a separate entity for the purposes of VAT (see Chapter 6 for a more detailed discussion of VAT).

3.7 DIVIDENDS-WITHHOLDING TAX

A dividend is an amount that a company can pay to its shareholders when the company has made a profit. The company in Example 3.13 would be able to pay a dividend of R5 760 to its shareholders. This is calculated as follows:

Example 3.13 – Calculating a dividend	
Taxable income (profit):	R8 000
Less tax paid to SARS:	R2 240
Dividend (profit retained in the company):	R5 760

There is, however, a dividends-withholding tax that is payable when a dividend is declared. This tax is 20% of the dividend amount. In the above example, a dividends-withholding tax to the amount of R1 152 will be payable to SARS (before the dividend may be paid out to shareholders). The effect on the amount shareholders receive would be as follows:

Example 3.14 – Calculating dividends-withholding tax	
Taxable income (profit):	R8 000
Less tax paid to SARS:	R2 240
Dividend (profit retained in the company):	R5 760
Dividends-withholding tax:	R1 152
Net dividend:	**R4 608**

When a company pays dividends to shareholders, the company is required to submit a dividends tax return to SARS. These returns are known as DTR01 and DTR02, and both must be submitted.

3.8 CAPITAL GAINS TAX (CGT)

It is important to distinguish between income that is revenue (income for services rendered or sale of trading stock) and income received upon the sale of a capital asset that has been held as an investment (capital income). For example, if your business purchases a building that your company operates out of, this will be a capital asset. If this building is sold, the sale may lead to a capital gain, which might result in CGT having to be paid. Capital gains are dealt with in a different manner to normal income tax. This is best illustrated by an example:

Example 3.15 – Calculating capital gain	
Purchase price of asset:	R500 000
Sale price of asset:	R700 000
Capital gain:	R200 000

A portion of this capital gain (80% for companies and 40% for an individual running a sole proprietorship) is added to your other taxable income and taxed accordingly. For a company, a capital gain of R200 000 will be taxed as follows:

Example 3.16 – Calculating CGT	
Capital gain:	R200 000
Inclusion rate of 80%:	R200 000 x 80%
Amount to be added to taxable income:	R160 000
Taxable income:	R160 000 (assuming no other taxable income)
Tax payable at 28% of R160 000:	R 44 800
Thus, CGT payable on the R200 000 gain in this example would be R44 800.	

The details of any capital gain will be reflected in your provisional tax calculations and your final tax return.

3.9 PROVISIONAL TAX

Provisional tax is not a separate type of tax but a form of collecting income tax: it is an estimate of the tax that the business will be liable for when the financial year is complete and is payable to SARS twice a year. People in salaried employment are generally not provisional taxpayers, but all companies and sole proprietorships are. All companies and all individual taxpayers that run a business as a sole proprietorship must register as provisional taxpayers with SARS.

A sole proprietorship will not need to register as a provisional taxpayer if their only business income is from the rental of fixed property and the taxable income from the properties does not exceed R30 000.

The reason for provisional tax is that, when a business receives income from a client, the client pays money to the business without deducting any tax first. Thus, a company or sole proprietor (unlike an individual who has PAYE deducted from the salary amount each month) does not pay tax on income each month. Instead, companies and sole proprietors pay provisional tax twice a year.

Companies and sole proprietors are required to submit a provisional tax return (IRP6) twice a year. The first return is due six months into the financial year and the second return is due on the last day of the financial year. For example, if your company has a February year end (as most South African companies do), the first provisional tax return is due at the end of August each year and the second provisional return is due at the end of February each year.

A provisional tax return is a return submitted to SARS based on an estimate of taxable income. So the amount of tax you need to pay in terms of the provisional return is based on your estimate. The provisional tax calculation is based on the same principles as the income tax calculation set out in section 3.1. A detailed provisional tax calculation is shown in Examples 3.17 and 3.18. It is important that an accurate estimate is made, as SARS will charge interest and impose penalties if you do not calculate your tax liability accurately enough. The general rule is that your second provisional tax calculation must be at least 90% accurate if your taxable income is less than R1 million, or 80% accurate if your taxable income is more than R1 million. This level of accuracy will usually ensure that you avoid paying penalties for underestimation of provisional tax.

All provisional tax payments made in terms of the IRP6 tax forms are considered when the business files its annual tax return

(ITR12). Provisional tax payments are offset against the business's total tax liability for the year. This avoids a situation where the business has to budget for a single, large tax payment at the end of the financial year. In fact, if provisional tax estimates are accurate, there may be no tax liability, or the company may need to pay only a minimal top-up amount upon submission of the annual tax return. Alternatively, if the estimated provisional tax payment was too high, SARS will refund any excess tax paid upon filing the annual tax return. In other words, instead of paying the full tax liability when filing its yearly tax return, the company pays tax by means of the provisional payments.

It is important to bear in mind that if a business is running at a loss (i.e. an assessed loss), it does not need to make any provisional tax payments. However, it still needs to submit a nil provisional tax return twice for that particular year. In such a case, it will not receive a refund from SARS. You are only entitled to a refund if you have overpaid tax. If there is an assessed loss, you will not have paid tax in the first place, so you cannot get a refund.

Examples of a provisional tax calculation for a company

Below is a sample calculation for the first provisional tax period, i.e. the first six months of the financial year, for a company:

Example 3.17 – First provisional tax payment: company	
Estimated gross income for the full financial year:	R40 000
Less estimated deductible expenses for the full financial year:	R10 000
Estimated taxable income:	R30 000
Tax at 28% on R30 000:	R 8 400

As this payment is for the first provisional tax period and the estimated tax payable for the full financial year is R8 400, you will pay SARS an amount of R4 200 (50% of R8 400) at the time the first provisional tax return is due, in August. Estimated gross income and expenditure are generally established by doubling the estimated income for the first six months. This is done because the company obviously cannot determine accurately what its income will be six months in advance.

Here is a sample calculation for the second provisional tax period, i.e. the full financial year, for a company:

Example 3.18 – Second provisional tax payment: company	
Estimated gross income for the financial year:	R60 000
Less estimated deductible expenses:	R20 000
Estimated taxable income:	R40 000
Tax at 28% on R40 000:	R11 200
Less first provisional payment:	R 4 200
Second provisional tax due:	R 7 000 (R11 200 – R4 200)

As the calculations are made at the end of the financial year, the company will be able to establish that its gross income is R60 000 (instead of the projected R40 000 in the earlier calculation), so it needs to make the necessary adjustment to the second provisional tax return.

Also, as this is the second provisional tax period, the full amount of estimated tax becomes payable (i.e. R11 200) with the filing of this return. This second amount payable will take into account all payments made in the first provisional period. When you submit your final tax return for the financial year, this amount paid will be used to reduce any tax that might still be owing. If you were able to estimate your provisional tax liability correctly, you may not need to pay any additional tax when you submit your final return. If you overpaid based on your provisional estimates, then you will be eligible for a tax refund from SARS.

Examples of provisional tax calculation for a sole proprietorship

For the sake of clarity, I use the same example as in the previous section to show how calculations differ between a company and a sole proprietorship.

Here is a sample calculation for the first provisional tax period, i.e. the first six months of the financial year, for a sole proprietorship:

Example 3.19 – Estimated taxable income: sole proprietorship	
Estimated gross income for the financial year:	R40 000
Less estimated deductible expenses for the financial year:	R10 000
Estimated taxable income:	R30 000

Instead of the taxable income being taxed at 28% (as for a company), the individual tax table (Table 3.1) is used. If you refer back to the table, you will see that taxable income of R30 000 falls into the first band of the individual tax table. The calculation will then be as follows:

Example 3.20 – Calculated taxable income: sole proprietorship	
Estimated taxable income:	R30 000
Tax payable:	R 5 400 (R30 000 x 18% = R5 400)
Less rebate	
(see Example 3.12):	R14 220
Total tax payable:	R 0

In this example, the sole proprietor would not need to pay any provisional tax (although he or she still needs to file a provisional tax return), as there is no tax due. But if the estimated taxable income is R200 000 (as per Example 3.12), then the calculation would be done as follows:

Example 3.21 – First provisional payment: sole proprietorship	
Estimated taxable income:	R200 000
Tax payable:	R 36 332
Less rebate:	R 14 220
Total tax payable:	R 22 112
First provisional payment due:	R 11 056 (R22 112 ÷ 2)

Remember that R11 056 is 50% of the total tax payable, as this is the payment for the first provisional tax period.

If we now presume that the taxable income is the same for the second provisional tax return, then the taxpayer would pay the remaining R11 056 at the end of the financial year, when the second provisional tax payment is due.

A business owner must therefore understand clearly that the business needs to pay tax twice a year – and not only at the end of the tax year, when the final yearly tax return is submitted. The business should therefore deal with income from its customers in such a way that it has the necessary cash flow available to pay tax due to SARS six months after the start of the financial year and again at the end of the financial year.

Chapter 4

EMPLOYEES' TAX

4.1 PAY-AS-YOU-EARN (PAYE)

Employers become liable to pay employees' tax when an employee of the business earns above the individual tax threshold. This employees' tax is known as pay-as-you-earn (PAYE). PAYE is not a separate tax; it is income tax that is levied on individuals in salaried employment. It is paid over to SARS before the employee receives their salary.

For the 2020 tax year, the tax threshold for individuals is R79 000 (if the individual is under 65 years old). This means that if an employee is paid less than this amount, the employer does not have to pay PAYE to SARS for that employee. If an employee earns above this amount, the employer needs to register with SARS and pay PAYE for this employee each month. The employer is then required to file a monthly EMP201 (PAYE tax return) via eFiling. Employers may be in a situation where they pay PAYE for some employees but not for others.

If the employer is liable to pay a skills development levy (SDL), discussed in section 4.3, then the employer also has to register as an employer with SARS. This may be the case even if no PAYE is payable.

As mentioned in Chapter 3 (see section 3.6), a sole proprietor does not need to register for PAYE unless he or she has employees whose salary is higher than the tax threshold.

4.2 UNEMPLOYMENT INSURANCE FUND (UIF)

The unemployment insurance fund (UIF) is a government-run fund that provides benefits to people who become unemployed or are unable to work due to illness, or who are taking maternity or adoption leave.

All employers are liable to contribute towards UIF for an employee unless an employee is employed for less than 24 hours a month. If the employer deducts PAYE for employees or is liable to pay the SDL through SARS, then the UIF contribution will be paid via the SARS PAYE payment channels; if not, the employer will need to pay UIF directly to the Unemployment Insurance Commissioner. The contribution amount payable is calculated as follows:

- the employee contributes 1% of his or her remuneration; and
- the employer contributes an amount equivalent to 1% of the employees' remuneration.

The employer must then pay over the total 2% contribution. The employee's 1% is deducted from his or her salary before the salary is paid over by the employer. The employer then pays both his own and the employee's UIF share over to SARS.

UIF contributions are based on a maximum salary of R14 872 per month per employee, which means that an employee will be required to contribute a maximum of R148.72 per month, even if the employee's salary is above R14 872 a month.

4.3 SKILLS DEVELOPMENT LEVY (SDL)

The skills development levy (SDL) is a government-imposed levy that is payable by employers. It is due on 1% of the total amount paid in salaries to employees if the employer pays (or expects to pay) salaries of more than R500 000 over a 12-month period. This amount will be paid via the SARS PAYE payment channels. Note that the SDL amount is included on the EMP201 returns that are submitted for PAYE.

Example 4.1 – Sample SDL calculation

When a business has employees who each earn a salary of R600 000 per year, the monthly SDL contribution payable by the company will be R500 per employee. As the monthly salary per employee is R50 000, the employer needs to pay over 1% of R50 000, i.e. R500 for each employee.

Chapter 5

SMALL BUSINESS CORPORATIONS AND MICRO BUSINESSES

5.1 SMALL BUSINESS CORPORATIONS (SBCs)

Companies (or CCs) that meet certain requirements can qualify as a small business corporation (SBC). This means that the company is taxed at reduced rates. The status of a company is not affected if it qualifies as an SBC; it is merely treated as an SBC when the tax return is filed to allow the company access to the reduced tax rates. A sole proprietorship cannot be an SBC.

Requirements for qualifying as an SBC

For a company to qualify as an SBC, it has to meet the following requirements:

- the shareholders of the company must be natural persons, i.e. sharcholdcrs cannot bc anothcr company;
- the shareholders may not hold shares in other companies (besides listed companies and some other lesser known types of companies);
- the gross income of the company may not exceed R20 million for the year of assessment;
- the company cannot generate more than 20% of its income (including capital gains) from investment income

and personal services (refer to the definitions of these terms in the text box).

However, note that a company can still qualify as an SBC if it provides personal services and if:

- the personal services offered are not performed by a person holding an interest in the company; or
- the company employs three or more unconnected full-time employees throughout the year.

In other words, a company may render legal services (which would normally be regarded as personal), but if it employs three or more people full-time, then it may still be able to qualify as an SBC. However, if a company is a personal service provider (for example, a security company that hires out staff to work at their clients' premises), that company is automatically disqualified from being awarded SBC status.

Definitions

Investment income: dividends, royalties or rental income derived from immovable property, annuities or similar income.

Personal service: any service that is rendered personally by an individual, for example, accounting, legal, education or architecture.

SBC tax rates

If a company qualifies as an SBC, the company will indicate this on its annual tax return. The company is then entitled to the tax rates shown in Table 5.1 (these rates should automatically be calculated by SARS upon submission of the return):

Table 5.1 SBC tax rates

Taxable income (R)	Rate of tax (R)
0–79 000	0%
79 001–365 000	7% of taxable income above 79 000
365 001–550 000	R20 020 + 21% of taxable income above 365 000
550 001 and above	58 870 + 28% above 550 000

Table 5.1 shows that quite a significant tax benefit is potentially available to companies that qualify as SBCs (compared to the 28% flat tax rate that usually applies to companies).

Example 5.1 – Sample tax calculation for an SBC

An SBC has taxable income of R400 000. This amount falls into the third band of taxable income. Thus, its tax liability is calculated as follows:

R400 000 – R365 000
= R35 000 x 21%
= R7 350

R7 350 + R20 020 (the amount of tax to be added as per the third band of taxable income)
= R27 370

Thus the total tax payable by an SBC on an income of R400 000 is R27 370.

Compare the calculation in Example 5.1 to the calculation for a private company that is taxed at 28%:

Example 5.2 – Sample tax calculation for a company
R400 000 x 28% = R112 000

A company that is taxed at a rate of 28% would pay tax to the sum of R112 000, while an SBC pays only R27 370. This is R84 650 less tax than a company taxed at the normal rate (R112 000 – R27 370 = R84 630).

Over and above this tax benefit, SBCs also benefit from accelerated wear-and-tear allowances for assets purchased. An SBC can deduct 50% of the cost of an asset in the first year of use, 30% in the second year and 20% in the third year.

In addition, if any plant or machinery purchased by the SBC is used directly in the process of manufacturing (except if the SBC operates in the mining or farming trade), it may deduct the full cost of that asset in the year the asset is brought into use.

5.2 MICRO BUSINESSES

A sole proprietorship, company, partnership or CC that has a qualifying turnover for the year of assessment of less than R1 million may register as a micro business and qualify for turnover tax. Qualifying turnover includes total receipts from carrying on business activities, but excludes amounts of a capital nature and exempt income.

Turnover tax

Turnover tax is a simplified form of taxation that applies to micro businesses. It combines the following types of tax:

- income tax;
- CGT;

- VAT;
- provisional tax; and
- dividends tax.

The primary difference between turnover tax and tax payable by any other business (other than a micro business) is that the tax for a micro business is paid on the turnover of the business, and not on the taxable income. A micro business does *not* use the normal formula for calculating income tax for businesses (see Chapter 3). Also, a micro business does *not* deduct from its income any deductible expenses; it pays tax on its *turnover.*

While it may sound as if this would result in higher tax payments, tax rates on turnover for a micro business are so low that this is often the best scenario for the micro business owner.

A micro business must file three tax returns each year that encompass all the above types of tax as one payment.

Registration as a micro business

A business can register as a micro business if:

- all its shareholders are natural persons (for a company);
- the owner of the sole proprietorship or company has no shares in other companies (other than listed companies and some other types of lesser known companies, for example, a body corporate);
- if a maximum of 20% of income is from professional services and investment income (the 20% investment-income limit does not apply to sole proprietorships or partnerships, but does apply to a company/CC);
- if the business is not a personal service provider or a labour broker;

- if the company has its year end in February;
- if the business does not have proceeds from the sale of property held as a capital asset exceeding R1.5 million in the current and two preceding years, i.e. three years; and
- if the business is a partnership and all the partners are natural persons.

A partner in a partnership may be disqualified from qualifying for turnover tax if that person holds shares in a company (either in a listed company or other, lesser-known types of companies), or is a partner in any other partnership. If a business earns less than R1 million in qualifying turnover and qualifies in terms of the above stipulations, it may register as a micro business with SARS. Unlike an SBC, a business that wishes to qualify as a micro business has to follow a formal registration process with SARS. The SARS guide for micro businesses provides more detailed information on registering your business as a micro business.

If an individual who runs his or her business as a sole proprietorship registers as a micro business, they will be liable to pay turnover tax based on the tax tables for micro businesses, and not in terms of the individual tax tables.

Tax rates for micro businesses

The tax rates for a micro business are set out in Table 5.2:

Table 5.2 Tax rates for micro businesses

Turnover (R)	Rate of tax (R)
0–335 000	0%
335 001–500 000	1% of each R1 above 335 000
500 001–750 000	1 650 + 2% of the amount above 500 000
750 001 and above	6 650 + 3% of the amount above 750 000

Example 5.3 – *Sample tax calculation for a micro business*

A micro business has taxable turnover of R400 000. Its tax liability is calculated as follows:

Turnover above R335 000 is charged at 1%:

R400 000 – R335 000

= R65 000 x 1%

= R650

Thus total tax payable on a taxable turnover of R400 000 is R650.

Bear in mind that it is difficult to compare this calculation for a micro business directly with the calculation for an SBC, as the SBC tax rate is based on taxable income and not on taxable turnover. Calculations will always vary, depending on the deductions available to the business. It is recommended that you conduct an analysis of your own business to determine whether a micro business or an SBC would be the better option for your particular business.

Chapter 6

VALUE ADDED TAX (VAT)

6.1 A SHORT OVERVIEW OF VAT

Companies that are registered as VAT vendors have to levy VAT on goods sold or services rendered to their clients. A company is not automatically a VAT vendor. To become a VAT vendor, it needs to file a separate application from registering for income tax. This can only be done if the company complies with certain requirements.

Input and output tax

Two aspects of VAT need to be clarified when dealing with VAT liability: output tax and input tax.

Output tax is the VAT that is levied by a company that is selling goods or supplying a service to clients. For example, if a company is a VAT vendor and charges a client R200 for services rendered, it must charge its client R200 + 15% output tax. The company will thus be required to charge the client R230. The output tax charged is R30.

Input tax is the VAT that is levied on goods or services that the company receives as part of the operation of their business; for example, if a company buys clothes from a third party that it resells, and this third party charges VAT on this sale. If the company has paid the third-party supplier R115, and R15 of this amount is VAT, the input tax that the company has incurred is R15.

Example 6.1 – Calculating VAT liability

---

1. A VAT vendor has to calculate its VAT liability to SARS. In the case of the figures mentioned above, the VAT liability would be calculated as follows:

Output tax – input tax = tax liability
R30 – R15 = R15

So the VAT vendor has to pay R15 VAT to SARS upon filing the VAT201 return, as output tax was R15 greater than the input tax.

2. A VAT vendor charges output tax to the sum of R700 to its clients. The same vendor has paid input tax to the sum of R560 on services supplied to it. What is the vendor's VAT liability, i.e. the amount that the vendor will need to pay over to SARS?
R700 – R560 = R140

Output tax is only paid to SARS once the VAT vendor's VAT return is filed. This will happen once a month, once every two months, once every six months or once a year, depending on the turnover and nature of the business; the return is called a VAT201 return. When a company charges VAT to a client, VAT amounts received will remain in the company account until the VAT return is filed.

The VAT system allows a VAT vendor to effectively reduce the amount of input tax payable to SARS by deducting input tax from output tax and paying over the difference.

If input tax exceeds output tax, SARS has to refund the VAT vendor for the amount.

6.2 REGISTRATION AS A VAT VENDOR

There are two types of VAT registrations: voluntary VAT registrations and compulsory VAT registrations. A person trading as a sole proprietor can register as a VAT vendor.

Voluntary VAT registrations

A company may choose to register as a VAT vendor if their taxable supplies (these are supplies that are subject to VAT, which includes zero-rated supplies) are R50 000 in the previous 12-month period or there is a contract in place to make taxable supplies to the sum of R50 000 in the following 12-month period.

Compulsory registration

A company whose taxable supplies exceed R1 million in any consecutive 12-month period, or a company that has a written contract in place to make taxable supplies exceeding R1 million within the next 12-month period, must register with SARS for VAT.

6.3 ADVANTAGES AND DISADVANTAGES OF REGISTERING AS A VAT VENDOR

Depending on the circumstances that apply to your business, it is not always advantageous to register for VAT (unless you are obliged to do so based on turnover). The following considerations should be taken into account when coming to the decision whether to register for VAT or not.

Advantages of registering as a VAT vendor

There are a number of advantages to being registered as a VAT vendor.

- The main advantage is that a company that is registered as a VAT vendor will have a reduced input tax liability, as it is able to deduct its input tax from any output tax that is levied. By contrast, if a company is *not* a registered VAT vendor, it will be paying VAT on the goods and services that are supplied to it, but it cannot reduce the amount of VAT payable to SARS by claiming the input tax.

Example 6.2 – Sample VAT calculations

1. For a company that is a VAT vendor:

Output tax charged to clients:	R30
Input tax charged by suppliers:	R30
VAT liability (output tax – input tax)	R 0

2. For a company that is not a VAT vendor:

Output tax charged to clients:	R 0
Input tax charged by suppliers:	R30

   This input cannot be claimed. VAT liability is R30.

- The output tax charged to clients is a cost to the company's clients and will not reduce its profit.
- If a company pays more input tax to its service providers than the output tax it charged its own clients, the company will receive a refund from SARS. For example, if the company purchased a large asset, the input tax on this could be claimed from SARS, resulting in a VAT refund.

- If immovable property is purchased from a vendor who is not registered for VAT, input tax can be claimed on the transaction (except in the case of property that the company buys to let out as residential accommodation).
- VAT registration enables a vendor to buy a business as a going concern without having to pay VAT on the transaction (thus making the purchase of a business cheaper).
- Finally, some businesses will require all companies that supply goods to them to be registered VAT vendors, so that they can claim input tax on supplies. This means that if you are not registered as a VAT vendor and wish to sell goods to a company that requires you to be a VAT vendor, they won't do business with you.

Disadvantages of registering as a VAT vendor

Some of the disadvantages of being a VAT vendor include that:
- a formal process has to be followed for registering as a vendor;
- VAT returns need to be filed every second month in the case of most companies;
- VAT makes your products and services more expensive to individuals or companies who cannot claim input tax (that is, to customers who are not registered VAT vendors).

SARS is in some instances entitled to refuse an application for a VAT registration – for example, if the business that is applying for VAT registration cannot produce proper accounting records, has no fixed place of business, or does not have a bank account.

It is important to bear in mind that companies that are not registered as VAT vendors may not charge output tax to their clients (and, in turn, are not entitled to claim input tax).

Goods that are imported into the country are also subject to VAT (at a rate of 15% on their value). In addition, imported goods are subject to customs duties. If goods are exported, the VAT vendor does not need to charge output tax.

6.4 VAT-EXEMPT AND ZERO-RATED SUPPLIES

Certain goods are either exempt from VAT, or zero-rated. Examples of *zero-rated* goods include petrol, exported goods, basic foodstuffs (such as fruit, vegetables, maize meal and brown bread). Goods that are *VAT-exempt* include financial services, public transport and residential accommodation. Note that zero-rated supplies have a 0% tax, but still form part of taxable supplies for the calculation to determine whether a company can apply for a voluntary registration or whether registration is compulsory. However, if your company only makes exempt supplies – for example, you own a bus company that transports people around South Africa – you are unable to register as a VAT vendor; the amount of your supplies will not make a difference.

Alternatively, your business may be supplying a combination of zero-rated and standard-rated supplies (taxable supplies). Standard-rated supplies have a 15% tax. For example, if you own a supermarket, you might sell both standard-rated supplies (for example, sweets) and zero-rated supplies (such as brown bread). If the combination of standard-rated and zero-rated supplies exceeds R50 000 in a 12-month period, you may apply to SARS to register as a VAT vendor. In the same vein, if your taxable supplies exceed R1 million, you are obliged to register as a VAT vendor.

Chapter 7

RENTAL PROPERTIES

There are many businesses that are in the trade of letting property. This may take the form of either a company that owns and lets property, or a sole proprietor (or partnership) that owns and lets property.

As many individuals are involved in the letting of property as an investment, the tax implications of doing so are worth considering separately here.

The letting of immovable property (such as a house) is considered a trade by SARS. Individuals who own a property and let it will have to deal with this trade separately in their tax returns. In terms of taxation, it is regarded as a separate business. If an individual taxpayer lets more than one property, each property is dealt with as a separate business in terms of taxation.

The trade of letting property is essentially based on the same principles as any other business. The owner has to calculate the rental income, deduct all applicable expenses incurred in respect of the rental property, and receive a profit (or loss) on this trade.

If the taxpayer makes a profit on the rental property, they will pay tax on this property; if they have made a loss, it will be dealt with as an assessed loss. SARS may try and ring-fence this loss; this is a rather complicated issue, but if your taxable income (excluding any assessed loss) does not attract the maximum marginal tax rate (45%), then a loss cannot be ring-fenced. You do not want your loss to be ring-fenced, as such a loss cannot be used to reduce taxable income from other trades you may be involved in. If your loss is not ring-fenced, it can be used to reduce your other taxable income; this can result in a reduction of your overall tax liability. For example, if you earn a salary and have a loss on a rental property that is not ring-fenced, the taxable income from your salary can be reduced by the assessed loss from your property rental (which will be calculated when you file your annual tax return each year) and result in a reduced tax liability.

Note that an assessed loss may only be ring-fenced if the taxpayer conducting the trade is an individual. However, if a company has an assessed loss from the rental property, it may not be ring-fenced.

The following are typical examples of rental-property expenses that may be deducted (note that this list is not exhaustive):

- bond interest (but not the actual capital repayments of the bond);
- repairs (but not improvements);
- garden services;
- maintenance;
- rental estate-agent commission;
- rates and taxes;
- body corporate levies; and
- cleaning services.

Here is a sample calculation of what a typical rental-property income/expenditure statement might look like for tax purposes:

Example 7.1 – Income/expenditure statement for a rental property

Rental income for the year:	R50 000
Less deductible expenses	
Bond interest:	R10 000
Repairs:	R 3 000
Garden services:	R 2 000
Rates and taxes:	R20 000
Total expenditure:	R35 000

Rental income less expenditure is therefore R15 000 for the year. This is the amount of profit (or taxable income).

This profit of R15 000 is taxed at a rate of 28% for companies (which would amount to a tax payment of R4 200). If the rental property belongs to an individual or sole proprietor, it is included in the person's taxable income. It is then taxed on the basis of the individual tax tables (see Table 3.1 on page 17).

Example 7.2 – Calculating tax on rental-income profit

If a taxpayer falls into the second band of taxable income, then the profit on the rental property in Example 7.1 will be taxed at 26%:

R15 000 x 26%

= R3 900

So a sole proprietor would be liable for a tax payment of R3 900 on a profit of R15 000.

If a taxpayer lets property as a sole proprietor and total taxable income from this property is R30 000 or more, the taxpayer will have to register with SARS as a provisional taxpayer and file two IRP6 returns per tax year, in addition to the normal ITR12 that needs to be filed each year.

Additional deductions for residential properties

Besides the deductions for expenses listed earlier in this chapter, taxpayers may deduct the cost of the actual property (5% of the cost per tax year) under very specific circumstances; for example, if a taxpayer owns five new and unused residential properties that are let as residential accommodation in South Africa (this excludes hotel proprietors or similar trades). If the unit is not free-standing (i.e. if it is an apartment), then only a portion of the cost may be deducted. The example below illustrates the benefit available to taxpayers if they qualify for this additional deduction.

Example 7.3 – Tax calculation for a free-standing residential unit	
For a free-standing residential unit that cost R500 000:	
Rental income:	R50 000
Less property expenses:	
(e.g. bond interest and rates)	R25 000
Less additional deduction (5% of cost of property):	R25 000
Taxable rental income for the tax year:	R 0

In Example 7.3, the taxpayer will not have to pay any tax on the rental income received from the residential accommodation. However, it is wise to bear in mind that there may be a recoupment of this additional 5% deduction if the property is sold at a later stage. This means that SARS will include the amount deducted in later taxable income. This recoupment greatly reduces the benefit that this additional deduction provides during the year of assessment for which the deduction is claimed.

Chapter 8

TAX RETURNS AND TAX CLEARANCE CERTIFICATES

8.1 TAX RETURNS

Companies and CCs are required to submit a tax return (ITR14) once a year. This tax return is submitted in addition to the two provisional tax returns that SARS requires of provisional taxpayers. Keep in mind that all businesses are provisional taxpayers. The ITR14 form reflects the finalised figures for the company or CC (based on financial statements that have been drawn up and finalised). The ITR14 tax return is due within 12 months after the financial year end of the company.

Individuals operating as a sole proprietorship must submit a tax return reflecting the income and expenses of their business on their individual tax return during the tax season. As stated earlier (see Chapter 1, section 1.2), individuals in partnerships will state the percentage of the partnership, along with the income and expenditure, on their individual tax returns.

- Entities that are registered as VAT vendors will also need to submit VAT returns to SARS.
- In addition, companies or CCs that declare a dividend must file a dividends tax return with SARS.

- A micro business must file three tax returns with SARS per financial year.

It is very important for a business to ensure that its tax returns are always up to date with SARS. If a business fails to submit its tax returns on time, it will become liable to pay interest and penalties to SARS. In addition, a business that is not up to date with its tax returns will not be able to obtain a tax clearance certificate, which might have further implications for its ability to carry out its operations.

8.2 TAX CLEARANCE CERTIFICATES

SARS can issue businesses and individuals who have a sole proprietorship or partnership with a tax clearance certificate (or TCC). This document confirms that the company or individual's tax affairs are up to date and that they have been compliant in terms of all tax regulations and all tax types, including income tax, VAT and PAYE. Companies will need a TCC when they apply for tenders. If all relevant tax returns have been submitted and the business or individual owes no tax to SARS, a TCC can be acquired from the SARS eFiling website. An individual or sole proprietorship will need a TCC if they wish to apply for tenders. Bank loans are also subject to TCCs.

CONCLUSION

'The opportunity is in the problem. The moment I see
a problem, I immediately begin to think about the
opportunities that can be created by trying to solve it.'
— **Strive Masiyiwa** (Zimbabwean
businessman and entrepreneur)

The tax implications of running a business are not widely
taught in the South African education system. This is why many
entrepreneurs are not well equipped to deal with the taxation
side of their businesses in an informed manner. The information in this book provides you with a basic understanding of
the different types of legal entities that are available to you to
run your business, and what the tax implications are for each
type of entity.

The practical examples in this book illustrate the differences
between running your business as a sole proprietor as opposed
to running your business as a company. This information will
help you decide what type of entity is most tax efficient in your
particular situation.

You now know what income tax, dividends tax, CGT, PAYE
and provisional tax entail, how to do VAT calculations, and
whether or not you should register your business for VAT. You

will also be in a position to decide whether your business may qualify as an SBC or micro business, which will give you access to reduced tax rates. And if you are in the business of letting property, an entire chapter explains how to maximise the tax advantages that are available for this trade.

Further information on the tax aspects of running a business may be found in various detailed SARS guides, listed in the Reference List at the end of this book. These guides go into greater detail about the topics that are covered in this book.

I would recommend that you discuss the various options presented in this book with your accountant or tax advisor to ensure that you choose the best entity for operating your business, so that you may access all available tax reductions.

It is my sincere hope that this book will give you the confidence to either start your own business or has provided you with greater insight into how to advance your business if you are already running one. Tax is one of the key elements of business. Access to all the relevant knowledge pertaining to tax will help you improve your business.

ABOUT THE AUTHOR

Daniel Baines is an admitted attorney with a Bachelor of Arts, LLB and MComm (in taxation) from Rhodes University. He completed his legal articles at Pagdens Inc. in Port Elizabeth, where he stayed for another year, running the firm's debt collection department. Daniel studied his MComm part-time while employed at Pagdens. After three years at Pagdens and completing his MComm, Daniel joined Grant Thornton as a tax consultant, where he worked for 15 months.

In April 2017, he joined PW Harvey & Co as a tax consultant and legal advisor. He currently works at Mazars as a tax consultant.

Daniel regularly contributes tax articles to *The Herald* newspaper and has had 12 of his tax articles published in the *Sunday Times*. Some of his most recent articles are:
- 'What to do if SARS does not pay out your tax refund' – *BusinessTech* 14 July 2018
- 'What to do if you have not filed your tax returns for years' – *BusinessTech* 21 July 2018
- 'After retirement taxman still takes a bite from your annuity' – *Sunday Times* 23 September 2018

- 'How to limit capital gains tax on the disposal of your property' – *Sunday Times* 7 October 2018
- 'How do I declare an allowance for work trips away from home?' – *Business Live* 11 November 2018

Daniel has had extensive experience dealing with taxation at Grant Thornton, PW Harvey and Mazars.

REFERENCE LIST

Most of the resources mentioned in this book are available from www.sars.gov.za – the website of the South African Revenue Service, or SARS, which is updated regularly.

- **Comprehensive Guide to Capital Gains Tax (Issue 5):** http://www.sars.gov.za/AllDocs/OpsDocs/Guides/LAPD-CGT-G01%20-%20Comprehensive%20Guide%20to%20Capital%20Gains%20Tax%20-%20External%20Guide.pdf
- **Comprehensive Guide to ITR12 for Individuals:** http://www.sars.gov.za/AllDocs/OpsDocs/Guides/IT-AE-36-G05%20-%20Comprehensive%20Guide%20to%20the%20ITR12%20Return%20for%20Individuals%20-%20External%20Guide.pdf
- **Department of Trade and Industry** website: available at www.thedti.gov.za
- **Guide on the Ring-Fencing of Assessed Losses arising from certain trades conducted by Individuals:** http://www.sars.gov.za/AllDocs/OpsDocs/Guides/LAPD-IT-G04%20%20Guide%20on%20Ring%20Fencing%20of%20Assessed%20Losses%20Arising%20from%20Trades%20Conducted%20by%20Individuals%20-%20External%20Guide.pdf
- **Income Tax Act No. 58 of 1962:** available at http://sars.mylexisnexis.co.za/#
- **Interpretation Note 1 (Issue 2) – Provisional Tax Estimates:** http://www.sars.gov.za/AllDocs/LegalDoclib/Notes/LAPD-IntR-IN-2012-01%20-%20Provisional%20Tax%20Estimates.pdf

- **Interpretation Note 28 (Issue 2) – Deductions of Home Office Expenses incurred by persons in employment or persons holding an office:** http://www.sars.gov.za/AllDocs/LegalDoclib/ Notes/LAPD-IntR-IN-2012-28%20-%20Home%20Office%20 Expenses%20Deductions.pdf
- **Latest tax rates:** http://www.sars.gov.za/Tax-Rates/Income-Tax/ Pages/Rates%20of%20Tax%20for%20Individuals.aspx
- Phillip Haupt *Notes on South African Income Tax 2018*
- **Tax Guide for Micro Businesses 2016/17:** http://www.sars. gov.za/AllDocs/OpsDocs/Guides/LAPD-TT-G01%20-%20 Tax%20Guide%20for%20Micro%20Businesses%20-%20 External%20Guide.pdf
- **Tax Guide for Small Businesses 2016/17:** http://www.sars.gov.za/ AllDocs/OpsDocs/Guides/LAPD-IT-G10%20-%20Tax%20 Guide%20for%20Small%20Businesses%20-%20External%20 Guide.pdf

ANNEXURE A

Sample tax comparison for a company, sole proprietorship and small business corporation (SBC):

EXAMPLE A – Company (no salary)		
Taxable income	R200 000	
Tax payable	R 56 000	
Profit retained in company	R144 000	
Less dividends tax	R 28 800	
Net dividend	R115 200	

EXAMPLE B – Company (with salary)			
Company profit		Director's salary	
Taxable income	R200 000		
Taxable income (less salary)	R 50 000	Salary	R150 000
Tax payable	R 14 000	Tax payable	R 27 000
Profit retained in company	R 36 000	Less primary rebate	R 14 220
Less dividends tax	R 7 200	Total tax payable	R 12 780
Net dividend	R 28 800	Net salary	R137 220
Net dividend + salary	R166 020		

EXAMPLE C – Sole proprietorship			
Taxable income	R200 000		
Tax payable	R 36 332		
Less primary rebate	R 14 220		
Net tax payable	R 22 112		
Net salary	**R177 888**		

EXAMPLE D – Small business corporation (SBC) (with salary)			
Company profit		Director's salary	
Taxable income	R200 000		
Taxable income (less salary)	R 50 000	Salary	R150 000
Tax payable	R 0.00	Tax payable	R 27 000
Profit retained in company	R 50 000	Less primary rebate	R 14 220
Less dividends tax	R 10 000	Total tax payable	R 12 780
Net dividend	R 40 000	Net salary	R137 220
Net dividend + salary	**R 177 220**		

SUMMARY	
Entity:	Amount owner receives:
Example A – Company (no salary)	R115 200
Example B – Company (with salary)	R166 020
Example C – Sole proprietorship	R177 888
Example D – SBC (with salary)	R177 220